HAL•LEONARD
INSTRUMENTAL
PLAY-ALONG

AUDIO ACCESS
INCLUDED

ALTO SAX

Piazzolla Tangos

To access audio visit:
www.halleonard.com/mylibrary

8226-3138-8085-1510

ISBN 978-1-4950-2841-0

BOOSEY & HAWKES

AN IMAGEM COMPANY

DISTRIBUTED BY

HAL•LEONARD®
CORPORATION
7777 W. BLUEMOUND RD. P.O. BOX 13819 MILWAUKEE, WI 53213

www.boosey.com
www.halleonard.com

AUSENCIAS
(The Absent)

ALTO SAX

ASTOR PIAZZOLLA

EL VIAJE
(The Voyage)

ALTO SAX

ASTOR PIAZZOLLA

CHANSON DE LA NAISSANCE
(Song of the Birth)
from FAMILLE D'ARTISTES

ALTO SAX

ASTOR PIAZZOLLA

MILONGA
from A MIDSUMMER NIGHT'S DREAM

ALTO SAX

ASTOR PIAZZOLLA

LIBERTANGO

ALTO SAX

ASTOR PIAZZOLLA

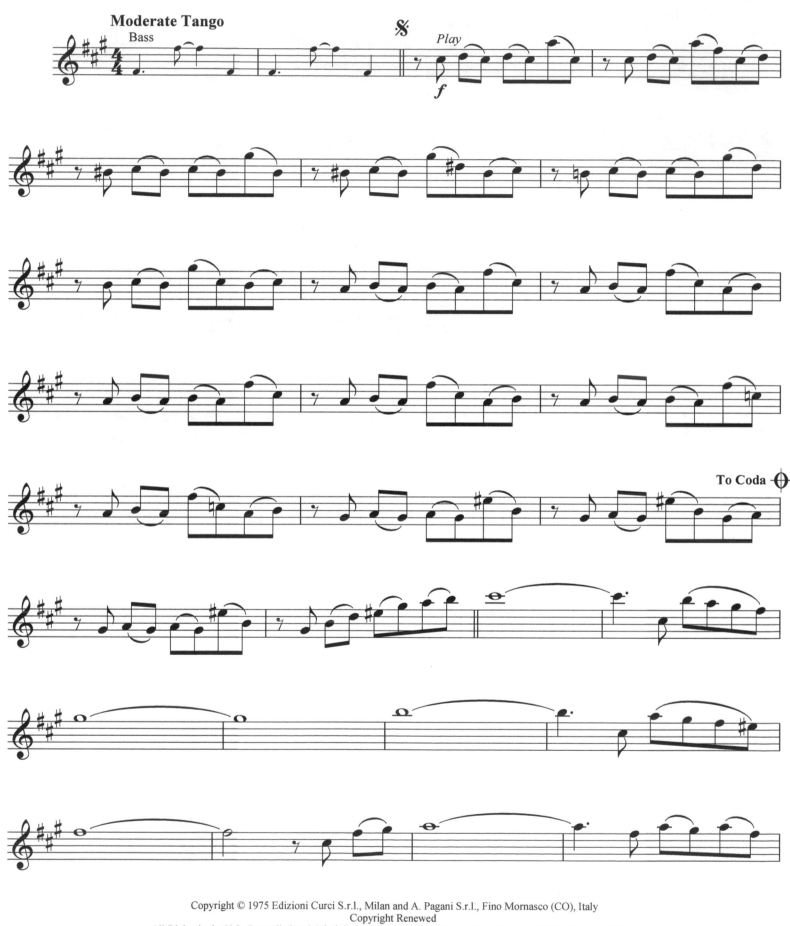

D.S. al Coda

CODA

LOS SUEÑOS
(Dreams)
from SUR

ALTO SAX

ASTOR PIAZZOLLA

OBLIVION

ALTO SAX

ASTOR PIAZZOLLA

OUVERTURE
from FAMILLE D'ARTISTES

ALTO SAX

ASTOR PIAZZOLLA

SENSUEL
(Sensual)
from A MIDSUMMER NIGHT'S DREAM

ALTO SAX

ASTOR PIAZZOLLA

SENTIMENTAL
from FAMILLE D'ARTISTES

ALTO SAX

ASTOR PIAZZOLLA

VUELVO AL SUR
(I'm Returning South)

ALTO SAX

ASTOR PIAZZOLLA

SIN RUMBO
(Aimless)

ALTO SAX

ASTOR PIAZZOLLA

STREET TANGO

ALTO SAX

ASTOR PIAZZOLLA

TANGO FINAL
from FAMILLE D'ARTISTES

ALTO SAX

ASTOR PIAZZOLLA